MW00977499

The Person

of the

Holy Spirit

The Person

of the

Holy Spirit

Being Filled with the Spirit of God

RHONDA MATTHEWS

Copyright ©2019 Rhonda Matthews

All rights reserved. Except as permitted under the U.S. Copyright Act of 1976, no part of this publication may be reproduced, distributed, or transmitted in any form or by any means, or stored in a database or retrieval system, without the prior written permission of the author.

Scripture quotations marked (AMP) are taken from the Amplified® Bible, Copyright ©2015 by The Lockman Foundation. Used by permission. www.Lockman.org

Scripture quotations marked (ESV®) are taken from The Holy Bible, English Standard Version®, Copyright © 2001 by Crossway, a publishing ministry of Good News Publishers. Used by permission. All rights reserved.

Scripture quotations marked (HCSB) are taken from the Holman Christian Standard Bible®, Copyright ©1999, 2000, 2002, 2003, 2009, by Holman Bible Publishers. Used by permission.

Scripture quotations marked (MEV) are taken from the Modern English Version. Copyright © 2014 by Military Bible Association. Used by permission. All rights reserved.

Scripture quotations marked (MSG) are taken from The Message. Copyright © 1993, 1994, 1995, 1996, 2000, 2001, 2002. Used by permission of NavPress Publishing Group.

Scriptures quotations marked (NIV®) are taken from The Holy Bible, New International Version®, Copyright © 1973, 1978, 1984, 2011 by Biblica, Inc.® Used by permission. All rights reserved worldwide.

Scripture quotations marked (NKJV) are taken from the New King James Version®, Copyright © 1982 by Thomas Nelson. Used by permission. All rights reserved.

Scripture quotations marked (NLT) are taken from the Holy Bible, New Living Translation, Copyright © 1996, 2004, 2007 by Tyndale House Foundation. Used by permission of Tyndale House Publishers, Inc., Carol Stream, Illinois 60188. All rights reserved

Cover Design by Carolynn Collins

Interior Design by Holly Murray

Editor Holly Murray

iv

A Note from the Author

This is my personal story about a subsequent event to salvation called the infilling of the Holy Spirit. It is also known as speaking in tongues or having a personal prayer language. The infilling of the Holy Spirit is available to every believer who has been born again.

It is my desire that, as you read this book, you will understand first and foremost that the infilling of the Holy Spirit is scriptural. It is different than salvation and has a different purpose. The infilling, or baptism, of the Holy Spirit adds a significant contribution to the effectiveness of the believer.

Second, I hope you understand that *you* can be filled with the Spirit of God and be given your own personal prayer language. It is a gift from God to all believers, and one with great purpose. As the church wakes to the fullness of its function in ministering to the needs of God's creation through the gifts of the Holy Spirit, we will see a tremendous impact on the world around us.

Contents

Chapter 1
It's in the Word

I'm a firm believer in knowing that everything we do is scriptural; that we find examples of what we are doing in God's Word. Because of that, there will be many Scriptures in this book to which I will refer so that you will have a firm foundation.

There are many Scriptures about the Holy Spirit (and what it means to be filled with the Holy Spirit) in the Word of God. In Acts 1:4, Jesus was telling His disciples what to expect when the Holy Spirit came in fullness on the earth. Verses four and five of Acts chapter one says:

> And while being in their company and eating with them, He commanded them not to leave Jerusalem but to wait for what the Father had promised, of which [He said] you have heard Me speak. *For John baptized with water*, but not many days from now you shall be baptized with (placed in, introduced into) the Holy Spirit. (AMP)

Baptized with the Holy Spirit? This was something new and different from what I grew up knowing, but there it was, in the Word of God.

As a child, I knew about water baptism. I had no idea when I was young, however, that the Word said to be baptized *with* the Holy Spirit. I did not know there was something more than my salvation package. But in this passage, we clearly see the words, "baptized in the Holy Spirit." It's in the Word.

Jesus also addressed speaking in tongues in the book of Mark, in a passage commonly known as "the Great Commission." Mark 16:15-17 (MEV) says:

> He said to them, "Go into all the world, and preach the gospel to every creature. He who believes and is baptized will be saved. But he who does not believe will be condemned. These signs will accompany those who believe: In My name they will cast out demons; *they will speak with new tongues*.

When we read this passage, we learn that Jesus is talking about speaking with new tongues. It's in the Word!

As a young adult, I learned that being baptized in the Holy Ghost, being filled with the Spirit, and speaking in tongues were all referring to the believer's privilege to have a personal prayer language and being able to speak in their heavenly language to God. The Word of God tells us we can pray in the Spirit and we can pray in the understanding. The Bible says, "Then what am I to do? I will pray with my spirit (by the Holy Spirit that is within me), but I will also pray (intelligently) with my mind and understanding" (1 Corinthians 14:15a, AMP). I knew that praying in my understanding meant that I was praying in English, my known language. I really wanted to learn what praying by the Holy Spirit meant in the Word.

Are you ready for the adventure of a lifetime that will give you a lifetime of adventure? Then get acquainted with the person of the Holy Spirit! Make it a habit to obey Him quickly. If you grieve Him, be quick to repent so that you can become sensitive to His leading again. Ephesians 4:30, in the Amplified version says:

> And do not grieve the Holy Spirit of God [do not offend or vex or sadden Him], by Whom you were sealed (marked, branded as God's own, secured) for the day of redemption (of final deliverance through Christ from evil and the consequences of sin).

That same verse in The Message translation reads, "Don't grieve God. Don't break His heart. His Holy Spirit, moving and breathing in you, is the most intimate part of your life, making you fit for Himself. Don't take such a gift for granted" (MSG).

Are you ready for the adventure of a lifetime that will give you a lifetime of adventure? Then get acquainted with the person of the Holy Spirit!

I grew up in a denomination where, when I heard the name "Holy Spirit," I did not connect the name with the fact that He is God. The only time I recall hearing the name "Holy Spirit" was in a baptism service. When the person was being baptized (dunked under the water), I would hear the preacher say, "In the name of the Father, the Son, and the Holy Spirit." I'm sure that I must have grieved Him for years by my lack of awareness that He was even there. If we are born again, the Holy Spirit lives in us. How sensitive we are to Him is up to us! He longs to communicate with us and for us to respond to His prompting.

How sensitive we are to the Holy Spirit is up to us!

We can't just live any old way we please and still have His precious promises operating in our lives to the degree He intends. But there is much that the Holy Spirit wants to share with us. First Corinthians chapter 2 is one of my favorite chapters in the Word of God. I love this chapter because it reveals things the Holy Spirit wants to show us. First Corinthians 2:9-10 (AMP) says:

> But on the contrary, as the Scripture says, what eye has not seen and ear has not heard and has not entered into the heart of man, [all that] God has prepared (made and keeps ready) for those who love Him [who hold Him in affectionate reverence, promptly obeying Him and gratefully recognizing the benefits He has bestowed]. Yet to us God has unveiled and revealed them by and through His Spirit, for the [Holy] Spirit searches diligently, exploring and examining everything, even sounding the profound and

4

bottomless things of God [the divine counsels and things hidden beyond man's scrutiny].

Do you see why I love that passage so much? There are things that God has prepared and keeps ready for those who love Him and obey Him. Did you notice this passage tells us these things are revealed through His Spirit? That is why it is so important to be sensitive to Him, to recognize when He is speaking to us, even when things don't make sense in our heads. He has great things in store for us, if we will recognize, listen, and obey His leading.

It is so important to be sensitive to the Holy Spirit, to recognize when He is speaking to us, even when things don't make sense in our heads.

After reading these Scriptures, I saw that there was a baptism apart from being baptized in water after asking Jesus in my heart. I also saw that a sign of a believer was to speak in tongues! I had grown up with a mindset that speaking in tongues was from the devil. Isn't that crazy? The devil is terrified of Christians tapping into this power! I was determined to learn more about the Holy Spirit and speaking in tongues. It was in the Bible, after all.

Chapter 2

My Story

As I began to search the Word, I saw very clearly that there is a subsequent event to salvation that can happen to a person who is born again. My journey to this revelation began when I got hungry for more of God. He answered the cry of my heart to know Him more and to love His Word. The result was my being filled with the Holy Spirit. Let me share my story with you.

My journey to the revelation about being filled with the Holy Spirit began when I got hungry for more of God.

I asked Jesus in my heart (got born-again/saved) in a little country church when I was six years old. Ron Drawdy, a young pastor in his early 20s, was the one who led me to Jesus. I loved Pastor Ron and his wife Joyce. He baptized me in water a few weeks later in a very old, outdoor baptismal pool. I had a special place in my heart for the man who had helped me to understand my need for Jesus and I decided that I wanted him to perform my wedding ceremony when I grew up.

When I was young, my mom would gather my family for nightly devotions. I loved this about my mom and still think she is most amazing! When we gathered for family devotions, my brother would play the piano for us while we sang and then we'd have a time of family prayer.

Mom was a rural mail carrier, and at the time the only Christian radio station was on the AM band. She listened diligently to Kenneth Copeland as he taught about this person of the Holy Spirit and about a prayer language which you could ask for. When I was 12 years old, mom came home after a day on her mail route and told me about hearing Brother Copeland teaching about speaking in tongues.

She told me that she asked the Lord to baptize her in the Holy Ghost. Then she told me that she heard this word – and it wasn't a word she knew. It wasn't English. She said that it had come up right out of her spirit, her inner being, and it was "other tongues." I told my mom that we just DON'T do that!

Many years later, coming out of another very predictable church service, I looked up at the sky and said, "God, I know you created me for more. Will you please show me how to grow in You?" At age 23, I became so hungry for more of the Lord.

I had attended church my whole life. I did not grow up in a church where there was a lot of freedom in the way we expressed our adoration of a loving heavenly Father. I hadn't been taught much of anything about the Holy Spirit, either. So, I understand where people are coming from when they don't understand the person of the Holy Spirit because I once was that person. This makes me particularly qualified to teach on this subject; I get what the confusion feels like.

I understand where people are coming from when they don't understand the person of the Holy Spirit because I once was that person.

I know if you look at me now, that might totally surprise you because you will often see me freely praising, lifting my hands, or anything else that I find evidence of in the Word. The church that I grew up in had a tradition that did not teach me that my hands were holy and to lift them to Him in praise. But in searching the Word, I read 1 Timothy 2:8, "In every place of worship, I want men to pray with holy hands lifted up to God, free from anger and controversy" (NLT). I continued searching the Word to see what else I might have been missing and wanted to find a church where I could learn even more about the Lord.

Pastor Ron Drawdy, the same man who had led me to Jesus when I was six and later married my husband and me, now pastored a church in Florida. He and his family had moved to Florida many years earlier, but my family had stayed in touch with them. The church he pastored was West Jacksonville Christian Center. In the 80s and 90s, I'd noticed the name "Christian Center" was a common name for Spirit-filled churches. Because I had felt something so different when I visited their church in Florida (it was the Holy Spirit I was sensing that was so different from what I was accustomed), I asked God to help me find a Christian Center where I lived in Georgia.

The next Saturday, I saw an advertisement for a newer church that was meeting in a YMCA building. My husband, Bryan, worked shift work. He would be working on that Sunday morning, so I asked a friend to go with me.

My friend and I walked into the church Sunday morning at 11:00 and everyone was already seated. There was no music playing, and the offering was about to be received. The pastor got up to speak, and I thought, "Wow! This seems like what I heard, felt, and saw from Pastor Ron at his church in Florida a few years ago!" I continued to attend for three more weeks, always arriving at 11:00 each Sunday morning. I thought it was so strange that there was never any music in their services, but the sermons preached from the Word were alive, and I was so hungry for the Word!

There was a woman who attended there named Linda Dunaway. Linda later became a mentor and spiritual mom to me, but after the third week of showing up at 11:00 a.m., she came to me and said, "Little friend, why do you come to church late each week?"

I asked her what time church started, and she told me that it began at 10:30 a.m.! I had been going at 11:00 a.m. because that was the traditional time that my denomination had always had church. I thought that was the time this Christian Center started church as well.

I realize now that the Holy Spirit had been protecting me. My traditions, my experiences in church to this point, were such that I would not have understood people lifting their hands. Until then, I had never read anything like this in the Bible, and that was no one's fault but my own.

I continued studying and searching the Word about tongues after I heard my pastor speak on a passage found in the book of Mark. Mark 16:17 says, "These signs will accompany those who believe: In My name they will cast out demons; they will speak with new tongues" (MEV). I thought, "I am qualified! I am a believer!" I became a student of the Word – not just picking out a verse here and there, but really studying it. If this prayer language was available, then I wanted to see it in the Word.

"I am qualified! I am a believer!"

After studying many verses in Scripture, I decided that I was ready to go all in. One evening, when Bryan was working the night shift, I got out my Bible. I cleared a space in my small closet. I moved the shoes and dresses out of the way. I put my hands up and said, "Lord, I believe this prayer language is for me. I'm ready!"

No sooner than I had prayed that prayer, I said, "WAIT! Not now! I don't want to be weird! What if I get a prayer language and start speaking in tongues, and my husband, Bryan, doesn't? We have had a good marriage, and what if this changes all that?" I left my closet without my prayer language.

When Bryan got home that night after midnight, he asked me about my evening. Bryan knew I had been searching the Word about speaking in tongues. I told him that I had changed my mind that night. In fact, I told him that I had gotten all worked up over it and, as a result, had a horrible headache.

Bryan and I had both heard our pastor speak about laying hands on the sick with the promise that they will recover. In fact, it was in the same section of Scripture that speaking in tongues was in! Mark 16:18b says, "they will lay hands on the sick, and they will recover" (NKJV). So even though neither of us spoke in tongues yet, we had the practice of laying hands on one another and praying any time we had any sickness attack our body. God honored our faith, and each time we were healed. This time was different. When he laid hands on me, the headache did not leave.

The next morning, I still had a headache! I had spent the previous evening going back and forth in my mind about the infilling of the Holy Spirit. Then I got a phone call from a Godly lady. She told me that the Lord had shown her that I had a really bad headache. I responded that I did, indeed! In my head, I was excitedly thinking, "Great! God has shown her and now she is going to pray about this headache and it is going to leave!"

Instead, she said, "The Lord showed me that you are worked up over the baptism of the Holy Ghost. He said you won't get a release from this until you are filled with the Spirit."

God honored our faith but also wanted me to know that He was hearing my prayers.

Oh, my goodness! I thought, "This is crazy!" She was right, but I had years of traditional church experience going through my head. It was filled with silly thoughts like, "What if Bryan and I don't get along because I start speaking in tongues? What if he thinks this won't be for him?"

Then the silliest of all thoughts came. I thought, "What if I can't wear lipstick anymore if I speak in tongues?"

As a child, the only time I saw people speaking in tongues was when I attended a Pentecostal church with my granny. Those ladies whirled and twirled, but they did not wear any makeup! Would speaking in tongues take away my lipstick?

The following morning, Bryan and I went to church. I still had a headache. The song service was going (I was there on time now thanks to Linda Dunaway telling me what time church started.). We were singing "El Shaddai" when the pastor interrupted the song. He said that the Lord had shown him that someone had been praying for God to fill them with the Holy Spirit.

The pastor said, "If you will just slip up your hands, He will fill you right where you are."

Wow! My God was so personal! He knew exactly what I needed to hear at that very moment. He knew the desire of my heart was for it to be a personal touch from Him. I had asked Him to fill me and He was serious about doing just that.

I put my hands up right there in the song service and heard (not in my head but in my innermost being) words that I never knew. Out of my mouth flowed other tongues. I did not draw attention to myself, but I did stand there weeping as I realized that God had answered my prayer and the headache was gone.

At the end of that church service, my husband went to the altar. One of the elders laid hands on him and Bryan was also filled with the Spirit. What a wonderful thing for the Lord to have done! The devil had tried to make me think that if I spoke in tongues, it might cause Bryan and me to not have a good marriage. But that was a lie from the enemy! The devil got defeated that November Sunday morning because Bryan and I both got filled with the Spirit on the same day!

Remember when I told my mom that we just DON'T speak in tongues? Eleven years had passed since she had shared with me about speaking in tongues and I had told her that. But now I had to call my mom and apologize. I told her,

"Yes! We DEFINITELY do this!" She had waited so patiently for me to find out for myself.

The gift of the Holy Spirit and speaking in tongues were definitely for us!

My studying and experiences assured me that this was not only biblical, but that it was from the Lord. Scripture confirms this. Acts 1:5 reads, "For John truly baptized with water, but you shall be baptized with the Holy Spirit not many days from now" (NKJV). And as I have earlier quoted, Jesus said in Mark 16:17, "These signs will accompany those who believe: In My name they will cast out demons; they will speak with new tongues" (MEV).

Chapter 3
Your Personal Prayer Language

M any times, you will hear the term "speaking in tongues" as though it was only one thing. But Mark 16:17 refers to tongues as a personal prayer language and is not the same as the gift of tongues that is mentioned in 1 Corinthians 12 and 14. The gift of tongues is one of the nine gifts of the Spirit which, when in operation, needs an interpretation. It operates as the Spirit wills. 1 Corinthians 12:4-11 says:

> There are diversities of gifts, but the same Spirit. There are differences of ministries, but the same Lord. And there are diversities of activities, but it is the same God who works all in all. But the manifestation of the Spirit is given to each one for the profit of all: for to one is given the word of wisdom through the Spirit, to another the word of knowledge through the same Spirit, to another faith by the same Spirit, to another gifts of healings by the same Spirit, to another the working of miracles, to another prophecy, to another discerning of spirits, to another different kinds of tongues, to another the interpretation of tongues. But one and the same

> Spirit works all these things, distributing to each one individually as He wills. (NKJV)

1 Corinthians 14:26-28 says:

> How is it then, brethren? Whenever you come together, each of you has a psalm, has a teaching, has a tongue, has a revelation, has an interpretation. Let all things be done for edification. If anyone speaks in a tongue, let there be two or at the most three, each in turn, and let one interpret. But if there is no interpreter, let him keep silent in church, and let him speak to himself and to God. (NKJV)

These passages both refer to the gift of tongues, requiring an interpretation in an understood language of what is prayed in tongues.

This book is specifically about having a personal prayer language and speaking in tongues as your private prayer language. The kind of infilling of the Holy Spirit to which I am referring in this book does not have to be interpreted, this is to benefit your prayer time.

It is very rare that you will hear us pray in our prayer language in a corporate setting (the church body together). The reason it is rare is that we do not want to bring confusion without an interpretation. But you may hear us speak in tongues when we don't know what else to pray in English.

An example of when we spoke in tongues as a personal prayer language in a corporate setting happened one Sunday morning during the sermon. The head of our security team was watching the service feed on a camera in the back of the sanctuary. They noticed there was a woman in the congregation who seemed to be struggling. They sent someone into the sanctuary to check on her, and as they were getting to her, she was falling out of her chair. When the security person got to her side, she was not breathing and there was no pulse. Several medical professionals were in the service and they began doing CPR and chest compressions.

Bryan was preaching while this was happening and was aware that this was a very serious situation. In fact, we later learned she had a heart attack. Mid-sermon, Bryan paused his teaching and began to pray in English. He did so for several minutes, but then he began to speak in tongues.

This was not the gift of tongues needing an interpretation. This situation was an example of the Scripture found in Romans 8:26, which says, "Likewise, the Spirit helps us in our weaknesses, for we do not know what to pray for as we ought, but the Spirit Himself intercedes for us with groanings too deep for words" (MEV).

The Spirit was helping Bryan to pray when he wasn't exactly sure how he should pray. He was limited in his own knowledge of the situation. He was also limited in his own language about what specifically needed to be addressed in prayer. Because of the baptism of the Holy Spirit, his personal prayer language allowed him to pray exactly what needed to be prayed at that moment. The Holy Spirit prayed through him.

*The Holy Spirit helps us to pray when we aren't exactly
sure how we should pray.*

This lady is alive today, after having had a heart
attack during service. I believe she's alive, not only because
we had smart and attentive medical professionals using their
natural gifts, but also because we have a pastor who knew he
needed assistance to pray what was needed. That assistance
was prayed in other tongues.

The first time anyone on Earth had been filled with a
prayer language is recorded in Scripture. You can find the
story about that in the book of Acts. Jesus had told His
disciples that the Holy Spirit would come upon them. Acts
1:8 says, "But you shall receive power (ability, efficiency,
and might) when the Holy Spirit has come upon you, and you
shall be My witnesses in Jerusalem and all Judea and
Samaria and to the ends (the very bounds) of the earth"
(AMP).

The Holy Spirit is in us to be a witness, to lead us,
and to show us things to come so that we know how to be
more specific in our prayers and in our decisions. I am one of
those people who believes we can walk close to the Holy
Spirit. If we are sensitive to Him and don't grieve Him, He
will show us where to go, where not to go, and protect us
always. We just need to listen to Him and follow His leading.

The Holy Spirit is in us to be a witness, to lead us, and to show us things to come.

Romans 8:14 says, "For all who are led by the Spirit of God are sons of God" (AMP). Two verses later, Romans 8:16, says, "The Spirit Himself [thus] testifies together with our spirit, [assuring us] that we are children of God" (AMP). So just by following those two Scriptures, you can really walk out His plan and know what you should and should not do.

Jude is a book of the Bible that only has one chapter. Jude verse 20 says, "But you, beloved, build yourselves up in your most holy faith. Pray in the Holy Spirit" (MEV). This Scripture is one of my main reasons for praying in the Spirit. My faith increases the more I pray in tongues - when I am using my personal prayer language. I'm a firm believer that many things I prayed about in other tongues years ago are things I am walking in today. This is such an exciting way to live!

My faith increases the more I pray in tongues - when I use my personal prayer language.

Jesus spent time teaching the disciples about the Holy Spirit when He was among them on Earth. Jesus shared with His disciples about the promise of the Holy Spirit in the book

19

of John. He said the Holy Spirit would come once He (Jesus) left the earth. John 14:16-17 says:

> And I will ask the Father, and He will give you another Counselor to be with you forever. He is the Spirit of truth. The world is unable to receive Him because it doesn't see Him or know Him. But you do know Him, because He remains with you and will be in you. (HCSB)

It is from these scriptures and others that we learn the nature of how the Holy Spirit operates.

Jesus further instructed His disciples, "But the Counselor, the Holy Spirit – the Father will send Him in My name – will teach you all things and remind you of everything I have told you" (John 14:26, HCSB). In John 16:7-8, Jesus said the following:

> Nevertheless, I am telling you the truth. It is for your benefit that I go away, because if I don't go away the Counselor will not come to you. If I go, I will send Him to you. When He comes, He will convict the world about sin, righteousness, and judgment. (HCSB)

And in John 16:13-14, Jesus told the disciples:

> When the Spirit of Truth comes, He will guide you into all the truth. For He will not speak on His own, but He will speak whatever He hears. He will also declare to you what is to come. He will glorify Me,

because He will take from what is Mine and declare it to you. (HCSB)

We see Jesus encouraging His very own disciples about the benefits for them personally when the Holy Spirit is released on the earth. The Holy Spirit would be many things to them. He'd be a counselor who would teach them and remind them of things Jesus had told them. The Holy Spirit is the Spirit of Truth and would guide them in truth. He would declare things to come. This was not just for Jesus's early disciples. This is for us, too, and we need the Spirit of Truth operating.

I have shared about the person of the Holy Spirit and some of the benefits I have experienced because of being filled with the Holy Spirit. I have also explained some of His purposes according to the Word, but I want to talk more about being filled with the Holy Spirit – especially regarding how *you* can receive this infilling of the Spirit.

Jesus spoke about perseverance in asking the Father for gifts in Luke 11:9-10. He said:

So I say to you, keep asking, and it will be given to you. Keep searching, and you will find. Keep knocking, and the door will be opened to you. For everyone who asks receives, and the one who searches finds, and to the one who knocks, the door will be opened. (HCSB)

It is good to know that He wants us to be persistent in asking Him for the gift of the Holy Spirit. He continued the

21

conversation by defining exactly what to ask the Father for in this manner. Jesus said in Luke 11:13, "If you then, who are evil, know how to give good gifts to your children, how much more will the heavenly Father give the Holy Spirit to those who ask Him?" (HCSB).

Our Father wants us to be persistent in asking Him for the gift of the Holy Spirit.

Our heavenly Father loves us and wants us to have the gift of the Holy Spirit. To receive this gift, you must first be a believer – you must have Jesus living in your heart. If He is your Lord and Savior, then you can ask for the infilling of the Holy Spirit – this event that comes after your salvation.

To receive the gift of the Holy Spirit, you must first be a believer.

While Jesus was still on Earth, He began to prepare others for what was going to be available to all who became believers. In John 7:37-39, He said the following:

On the last and most important day of the festival, Jesus stood up and cried out, "If anyone is thirsty, he should come to Me and drink! The one who believes in Me, as the Scripture has said, will have streams of living water flow from deep within him." He said this about the Spirit. Those who believed in Jesus were

> going to receive the Spirit, for the Spirit had not yet
> been received because Jesus had not yet been
> glorified. (HCSB)

Jesus was letting these people know that if they were thirsty for Him, then they could have this power. He was planting seeds in the hearts of the listeners, letting them know there was more coming.

Chapter 4

Be Filled

In the book of Acts, Jesus told His disciples to wait in Jerusalem for the outpouring of the Spirit. Acts 1:4 says, "Being assembled with them, He commanded them, 'Do not depart from Jerusalem, but wait for the promise of the Father, of which you have heard from Me'" (MEV). He then continued by explaining in verse 5, "For John baptized with water, but you shall be baptized with the Holy Spirit not many days from now" (MEV).

Those first believers had no idea what this was going to look or sound like. They did have an expectation, however, and we find in Scripture a written description of the event. Acts chapter 2 says:

> When the day of Pentecost came, they were all together in one place. Suddenly a sound like the blowing of a violent wind came from Heaven and filled the whole house where they were sitting. They saw what seemed to be tongues of fire that separated and came to rest on each of them. All of them were filled with the Holy Spirit and began to speak in other tongues as the Spirit enabled them. (Acts 2:1-4, NIV)

This scripture explains that they were filled with the Holy Spirit and the result was that they spoke in tongues.

People undoubtedly thought they were crazy! Acts 2:12 describes the emotions of the witnesses to this event. It says, "Amazed and perplexed, they asked one another, 'What does this mean?'" (NIV). They had never seen anything like this before!

Peter, one of Jesus' disciples who'd been filled with the Holy Spirit, explained what they were witnessing. Acts 2:14-18 says:

> Then Peter stepped forward with the eleven other apostles and shouted to the crowd, "Listen carefully, all of you, fellow Jews and residents of Jerusalem! Make no mistake about this. These people are not drunk, as some of you are assuming. Nine o'clock in the morning is much too early for that. No, what you see was predicted long ago by the prophet Joel: 'In the last days,' God says, 'I will pour out my Spirit upon all people. Your sons and daughters will prophesy. Your young men will see visions, and your old men will dream dreams. In those days I will pour out my Spirit even on my servants – men and women alike – and they will prophesy.'" (NLT)

The entire chapter goes on to tell what to expect in the last days. The people who heard him asked what they needed to do, and Peter answered them. His response is recorded in Acts 2:38 and says, "'Repent,' Peter said to them, 'and be baptized, each of you, in the name of Jesus Christ for the forgiveness of your sins, and you will receive the gift of the Holy Spirit'" (HCSB).

In the following verse, he explains that this promise is for them and for the children, "and for all who are far off, as many as the Lord our God will call" (Acts 2:39, HCSB). Because of his message to them, many believed and were baptized. Acts 2:41 (NLT) says about 3,000 people were added to the church that day.

Acts 2:42 says, "All the believers devoted themselves to the apostles' teaching, and to fellowship, and to sharing in meals (including the Lord's Supper) and to prayer" (NLT). The state in which our country currently finds itself is because the church has let a lot of things slip. There aren't many who will devote themselves first and foremost to the Word, to being in church, and to spending time in prayer. I am believing that the body of Christ is waking up to the seriousness of the hour. Picking these assignments back up and taking them seriously will yield great results personally. We can change communities, our country, and our world.

Believers need to devote themselves to reading and studying the Word of God, attending church, and spending time in prayer.

The behaviors of the early church led to remarkable results. Acts 2:43 says, "A deep sense of awe came over them all, and the apostles performed many miraculous signs and wonders" (NLT). In the same chapter, verse 47 says, (they were) "praising God and having favor with all the people. And every day the Lord added to them those who were being saved" (HCSB). There is a powerful truth found in this passage. If we will be serious with all that the Word tells us is available and we adjust our lives to really *do* what Matthew 6:33 says, "But seek first the kingdom of God and His righteousness, and all these things will be provided for you" (HCSB). What difference might we make around us?

We would make quite an impact if we would get serious with all that the Word of God says is available to us.

The greatest joy to us all should be when we see what happened in Acts 2:47, "And the Lord kept adding to their number daily those who were being saved" (AMP). All of this happened when the early church was established and filled with the promise of the infilling of the Holy Spirit. It is my prayer that we would be filled and impact our world in such a way that we all lead many to the saving knowledge of Jesus Christ.

All through the book of Acts, you can read about the works of the infilling of the Holy Spirit. Despite the enemy at work to inhibit the spread of the good news, the apostles shared about the life, death, and resurrection of Jesus even beyond their own town of Jerusalem. Acts chapter 8 begins by talking about a man named Saul. He had been present when Stephen, a believer, was martyred, and he spent much time persecuting the believers of Jesus, the church body in Jerusalem.

But even as Saul was "ravaging the church" (Acts 8:3, HCSB), the good news of Jesus was being preached to crowds in Samaria. Many were healed and delivered. When the apostles in Jerusalem heard about all that was happening in Samaria, they sent Peter and John to them. Acts 8:15b-16 explains why they were sent, "so that the Samaritans might receive the Holy Spirit. For He had not yet come down on any of them; they had only been baptized in the name of the Lord Jesus" (HCSB). But when Peter and John arrived and laid hands on them, they received the Holy Spirit.

In the next chapter of Acts, we learn of Saul's conversion to Christ. While on the road to Damascus, he encountered the voice of the Lord and was blinded. In the meantime, the Lord spoke to Ananias, a disciple who lived in Damascus. God told Ananias to go to a specific location and ask for Saul of Tarsus.

I can imagine that Ananias may have felt much concern in obeying the Lord because he knew who Saul was and what he had been doing to believers. But Ananias obeyed the Lord's command. Acts 9:17 tells us Ananias left where he was and went to where Saul was staying and placed his hands on him. Ananias told Saul, "Brother Saul, the Lord Jesus, who appeared to you on the road you were traveling, has sent me so that you can regain your sight and be filled with the

28

Holy Spirit" (HCSB). Verse 18 tells us "something like scales fell from his eyes, and he regained his sight. Then he got up and was baptized" (HCSB).

We learn that Saul spent time with the disciples in Damascus and then began telling others about Jesus. What a powerful change of heart! It didn't matter what Saul's past had been – receiving Jesus and the gift of the Holy Spirit changed his life! Acts 13:9 (HCSB) tells us that Saul, who was also called Paul, was a man who was filled with the Holy Spirit. Scripture tells us in Acts 19:11-12, "God did extraordinary miracles through Paul, so that even handkerchiefs and aprons that had touched him were taken to the sick, and their illnesses were cured, and the evil spirits left them" (NIV).

No matter your past, the gift of the Holy Spirit is for you.

Peter was a disciple who was also used mightily by God. In Acts 4:8, Peter, who was filled with the Holy Spirit, was able to boldly answer those who were questioning the miracles he and the other apostles were doing in Jesus' name. Acts 4:13 describes the reaction of the council:

> The members of the council were amazed when they saw the boldness of Peter and John, for they could see that they were ordinary men with no special training

in the Scriptures. They also recognized them as men
who had been with Jesus. (NLT)

Stephen, also, was full of the Holy Spirit. Acts 6:5b says,
"They chose Stephen, a man full of faith and of the Holy
Spirit" (NIV). Scripture tells us he was "full of God's grace
and power, (and) performed great wonders and signs among
the people" (Acts 6:8, NIV). When he faced opposition, the
Holy Spirit gave him the wisdom to answer those who were
arguing with him. Acts 6:10 says, "But they could not stand
up against the wisdom the Spirit gave him as he spoke"
(NIV).

*Being filled with the Holy Spirit will give you Godly
boldness and wisdom. You will have what you need
when you need it.*

God so needs the church to once again get this
passion for Him and get back to being *full of the Holy Spirit*.
When is the last time you shared your faith with someone or
when someone saw something in you that was different? I
say that as a challenge, not as condemnation. There needs to
be something in us that is different, something in us that
helps others to see it is Jesus in us. John 16:8 says, "And He,
when He comes, will convict the world about (the guilt of)
sin (and the need for a Savior), and about righteousness, and
about judgment" (AMP).

It is when we shine for Jesus, when we are walking in the power of the Holy Spirit, that others take notice. The purpose of this isn't to draw attention to ourselves, but to draw out an awareness in others of their need for Jesus. This is, after all, the Great Commission!

It is when we shine for Jesus, when we are walking in the power of the Holy Spirit, that others take notice.

There is an example of this in Acts 11. Peter shared the gospel with the Gentiles for the first time and they were filled with the Holy Spirit. Acts 10:34-48 tells of this event. It says that Peter was sharing the Gospel message of Jesus and of the miracles Jesus had performed. He was also telling about Jesus's death and resurrection and that they had been witnesses of all of that. While Peter was sharing this, the Holy Spirit fell on those who were listening. Acts 10:45-46 says, "The circumcised believers who had come with Peter were astonished that the gift of the Holy Spirit had been poured out even on Gentiles. For they heard them speaking in tongues and praising God" (NIV).

Because of the Holy Spirit being received by the Gentiles, with evidence of speaking in tongues, word spread. The Word tells us in verse 26 of Acts 11 that it was in this town where Barnabas and Peter were teaching crowds of people for a year that these believers were first called Christians. But it was a result of Peter sharing with the

Gentiles (who were filled with the Holy Spirit) that caused so many to take notice from the start. Acts 11:22-24 tells us the following:

> The report of this came to the ears of the church in Jerusalem, and they sent Barnabas to Antioch. When he came and saw the grace of God, he was glad, and he exhorted them all to remain faithful to the Lord with steadfast purpose, for he was a good man, *full of the Holy Spirit and of faith.* And a great many people were added to the Lord. (ESV)

Isn't this our whole purpose for being alive – to bring people out of darkness? We need to shine the love of Jesus and live for Him in such a way that He is revealed. We need to walk in the power of the Holy Spirit so that lives are changed and drawn to Jesus. The church body has been distracted for so long, but I believe this is the hour for the church to wake up. The key for the church to make a tremendous impact on the world is being filled with the Spirit. It is when we are full of the Holy Spirit that I see massive numbers being added to the church once again.

The book of Revelation says many times, if any man has an ear to hear, let him hear what the Spirit of God is saying to the church. The Holy Spirit is talking to us. Have we developed the ability to hear Him and obey?

I quoted Jude 20 earlier and will close this book with this verse as one of the best reasons to use your prayer language often. "But you, beloved, build yourselves up in

your most holy faith. Pray in the Holy Spirit" (Jude 20,
MEV). I personally feel that most of the promises I am
walking in today and will walk in tomorrow reflect my
making it a daily habit to pray in tongues and build up my
faith.

> *"But you, beloved, build yourselves up in your most*
> *holy faith. Pray in the Holy Spirit."*
> *(Jude 20 MEV)*

The person of the Holy Spirit is for you. He, like
salvation, is a gift received by faith. Ask for this amazing gift
for yourself and be filled with the Spirit.

Prayer

As His child, your loving Heavenly Father wants to give you the supernatural power you need to live this new life. He wants every believer to be filled with the Holy Spirit and speak in other tongues. You can pray and receive the baptism in the Holy Spirit just as you received Jesus – by faith, by believing God's Word. You are His child and He is your Father. God is ready to baptize you in His Holy Spirit when you ask Him. All you must do is ask, believe, and receive!

Simply repeat this prayer out loud:

> *Dear Heavenly Father,*
>
> *I come to You in the name of Jesus. I recognize my need for Your power to live my life and I desire to be baptized with Your Holy Spirit with the evidence of speaking in other tongues. Your Word says I can have it and I believe what You have said.*
>
> *Please fill me with Your Holy Spirit and, by faith, I receive Him right now! I thank you, Father, that I am baptized with the Holy Spirit with the evidence of speaking in other tongues! Holy Spirit, you are welcome in my life.*
>
> *In Jesus's name,*
>
> *Amen*

That's it! You have received the baptism in the Holy Spirit! Now it is possible that you didn't feel anything. Your receiving the Holy Spirit has nothing to do with feelings, however, or what happens on the outside. God's Word said that if you asked, you would receive. That means by faith you have received the baptism of the Holy Spirit.

Practice speaking in other tongues. It doesn't matter if you start with one syllable. It doesn't matter how silly you think you sound, either! Just keep praying and God will strengthen you in your prayer language.

There are many people who receive the baptism in the Holy Spirit and do not pray in tongues right away. Know that God is faithful to His Word. Luke 11:10 says, "For everyone who asks, receives. Everyone who seeks, finds. And to everyone who knocks, the door will be opened" (NLT). Verse thirteen of the same book and chapter reads, "If you sinful people know how to give good gifts to your children, how much more will your heavenly Father give the Holy Spirit to those who ask Him" (NLT).

Don't be discouraged, it will come. Just don't give up! Being filled with the Spirit of God will be the adventure of a lifetime that never has to end! The person of the Holy Spirit is a gift for you.

About the Author

We all need people in our lives who "bring out the gold" in us. Rhonda Matthews is such a person. She sees the God-given potential in every person she meets and invests her time drawing out that potential. She is quite optimistic and sees life through the eyes of faith. Because of this, she has touched the lives of many people with her wisdom, experience, and encouragement.

If there is anyone qualified to write a book on the Holy Spirit, it's Rhonda. Through 30 years of personal experience and the study of God's Word, she has discovered how to live a life following the voice of the Holy Spirit. She walks what she talks.

She and her husband Bryan are the lead and founding pastors of New Life Church in Augusta, Georgia. She has a previously published book, Prayer – A Holy Occupation, in which she chronicles several miracles God worked on behalf of their ministry. Bryan and Rhonda have one son, Carter, who is married to Elizabeth Ann.

Thank you for your support of this ministry. It is Rhonda's desire to encourage you to develop a deep relationship with the Holy Spirit and live victoriously surrendered to Him. If this book has helped you gain a deeper understanding of the person of the Holy Spirit, please rate this book online and share about it with others.

Made in the USA
Columbia, SC
21 June 2024

37091304R00024